Kipling's Soldiers

Kipling's Soldiers

A selection of Rudyard Kipling's poems
illustrated with paintings by

Bryan Fosten

Compiled, introduced and annotated by

George and Christopher Newark

The Pompadour Gallery

First published in Great Britain in 1993 by
The Pompadour Gallery
PO Box 11
Romford, Essex, RM7 7HY

Introduction © 1993 George & Christopher Newark.
Paintings © 1993 The Pompadour Gallery/Bryan Fosten,
Reprinted 1996

British Library Cataloguing in Publication Data.
A Catalogue record for this book is
available from the British Library.

ISBN 0 9519342 0 1

Set in New Baskerville by
Pennington Designs Limited,
Gidea Park, Essex
Printed in Hong Kong
by Bookbuilders Ltd

Contents

LIST OF PAINTINGS

INTRODUCTION

Rudyard Kipling was born in Bombay, India, in 1865 and after an education in England at the United Services College, Westward Ho! he returned to India to work on the *Civil and Military Gazette* at Lahore. It was there in the cantonments that Kipling came to know the men of the various regiments of the British Army stationed in India, particularly the private soldiers. He realised that they had their side of the story to tell of service in Queen Victoria's army and took it upon himself to make sure their voice was heard through his ballads. The popularity of his stories and verse undoubtedly prompted Victorian Britain to question its contemptuous attitude to the 'other ranks' of the army. His literary output was prodigious and in 1907 he became the first Briton to be awarded the Nobel Prize for Literature. After his only son John was killed in action serving with the Irish Guards in The Great War, Kipling worked devotedly for the War Graves Commission and was one of the originators of the nightly sounding of the Last Post at the Menin Gate, and the burial of the unknown soldier in Westminster Abbey. Rudyard Kipling died in 1936 and was honoured with burial in Poets' Corner, Westminster Abbey.

In this book we have endeavoured to match Kipling's ballads with paintings by Bryan Fosten to produce an authentic representation of 'Kipling's Soldiers'. Kipling had certain regiments in mind when writing his verse: The Queen's Own Corps of Guides in *The Ballad of East and West;* The Royal Artillery in *Ubique;* The Royal Engineers in *Sappers,* and The Royal Marines in *Soldier and Sailor Too* are some of the defined links. We have positioned figures of other regiments in the settings of Rudyard Kipling's poems and Bryan Fosten has depicted them in contemporary uniforms. Our efforts are two-fold; to show the many admirers of Kipling's work how his characters would have looked, and to add a further dimension to Bryan Fosten's paintings for the devotees of his military art. This project stems from the set of six postcards we published in 1988 on the theme of 'Kipling's Soldiers', and the many requests we have since had to extend the series. This prompted us to commission a further 18 paintings and we now present all 24 plates illustrating a selection of Kipling's ballads, augmented with black and white drawings and photographs of the period. No artist, to our knowledge, has illustrated Kipling's verse by utilizing a life-time study of military uniforms. In Bryan Fosten we have a gifted artist and meticulous researcher who, combined with our selection and origination will, we are sure, fill that void.

The concept of matching Kipling's words and characters with pictures has been explored before, not least by the motion picture industry. Some notable Hollywood productions were *Wee Willie Winkie* (20th Century-Fox 1937) with Shirley Temple, no less, in a change of gender for the title character; *Captains Courageous* (MGM 1937) with Spencer Tracy and Freddie Bartholomew; *The Light That Failed* (Paramount 1939) with Ronald Colman as Dick Heldar, and *Gunga Din* (RKO 1939) – a rip-roaring vehicle for Victor McLaglen, Cary Grant and Douglas Fairbanks Jnr. , with Sam Jaffe in the title role. Although this film bore little resemblance to Kipling's poem it began and ended with British actor Montagu Love reciting passages from *'Gunga Din'*. Later came *The Jungle Book* (United Artists 1942) with Sabu as Mowgli; *Kim* (MGM 1950) with Errol Flynn as Mahbub Ali, and *Soldiers Three* (MGM 1951) with Stewart Granger, Robert Newton and Cyril Cusack. *The Man Who Would Be King* (Columbia/UA 1975) starred Sean Connery and Michael Caine as ex-Sergeants Dravot and Carnehan, with Christopher Plummer giving an unerring cameo performance as Rudyard Kipling.

Music has also been used to complement Kipling's words, a throwback to the time when he wrote verse to match the metre of traditional army songs heard in India, and the roistering ballads he listened to at Gatti's Music Hall opposite his lodgings in Villiers Street, off the Strand, in London in 1890. In the 1920's and '30's Australian baritone Peter Dawson recorded many of the popular ballads set to music, *'Mandalay'* and *'Boots'*, particularly, becoming firm favourites played on gramophones up and down the country. Even Frank Sinatra had a stab at *'Mandalay'* singing an up-beat version on his album *Come Fly With Me* (Capitol 1957). It is said that the then copyright holder of the ballad, Kipling's daughter Elsie, was far from pleased with Sinatra's swinging rendition. Folk singer Peter Bellamy, who tragically died in 1991 aged 48, recorded a unique version of *Barrack-Room Ballads* in 1985 (Free Reed 014) set to the music of traditional English folk songs, which included an ingenious coupling of *'Gunga Din'* sung to the time-honoured Liverpool air *'Maggie May'*. Sir C. Aubrey Smith (1863-1948), the distinguished British actor long domiciled in Hollywood, and erstwhile England cricket captain, was also an excellent musician and, according to his obituary in The Times, set 'Barrack-Room Ballads' to music.

Early in his career the stage helped to bring Kipling's words to life with actors reciting his verse, billed as "dramatic monologues", in Victorian and Edwardian music halls. Delivered in sonorous tones with theatrical gestures emphasizing the actions, they undoubtedly helped to popularize Kipling's ballads. In recent times many writers, producers and directors have drawn on Kipling's work for inspiration. The National Theatre mounted a play at the Lyttelton in 1977 titled Soldiers Three in which Derek Newark, Warren Clarke and Kenneth Cranham dramatically interpreted 'Barrack-Room Ballads'. Actor Alec McCowen toured Britain in the 1980's with a one-man show reading and dramatising the books and ballads. Tony Perrin adapted Kipling and staged a show at the New Victoria Theatre, Stoke-on-Trent in 1990, also called Soldiers Three, with seven actors dramatising or narrating the verse, and Peter Bellamy "nasally warbling Kipling's ballads to a squeeze-box" as one critic reported. BBC Radio Four broadcast poems chosen and presented by Marghanita Laski to illustrate Kipling's English History, and BBC Television produced a Kipling series featuring Joss Ackland.

With a few notable exceptions the matching of Kipling's ballads with paintings seems to have been neglected by British artists. His books were initially illustrated by his father, John Lockwood Kipling, who produced some very capable drawings for the early publications distributed in India in the 1880's. The most enduring illustration of a Kipling ballad is without doubt 'A Gentleman in Kharki' by Richard Caton Woodville (1856-1927) drawn in 1899 to illustrate a broadside of 'The Absent-Minded Beggar' a verse penned by Kipling to raise money for the dependents of British soldiers fighting in South Africa. Among the finest artistic interpretations of Kipling's work are the evocative paintings by 'Snaffles' (Charles Johnson Payne,1884-1967) an ex-gunner and great admirer of Kipling who used quotations from the ballads to caption many of his paintings published as prints. Recent books with illustrations matching Kipling's verse have been Gunga Din (J. M. Dent & Sons 1987) containing numerous naive paintings by Robert Andrew

Parker illustrating this one poem, and *Moon of Other Days: M. M. Kaye's Kipling* (Hodder & Stoughton 1988) with some fine illustrations by George Sharp.

Bryan Fosten was born in 1928, the son, and grandson, of master military embroiderers. His father worked for a time in the studio of Fortunio Matania and Sir Septimus Scott, and he posed for the figures on the Royal Artillery Memorial at Hyde Park Corner, sculpted by Charles Sargeant Jagger. Bryan was apprenticed to the printing trade as a compositor in 1942, joined the British Army in 1946 and served in Italy, Egypt and Palestine. When demobilised, he returned to the printing industry to complete his training and studied at the London College of Printing and Camberwell School of Art, gaining his City and Guilds Certificate in 1950. Promoted through a printing workshop to manager, he entered publishing as a production manager on a technical newspaper, then became a freelance printing consultant. In 1973 he left the printing industry to become a full-time artist specializing in historical uniforms of the British Army, a subject he has studied for the past 50 years. In 1964 he was appointed founder-editor of *Tradition* magazine, that late-lamented inspiration of Roy Belmont-Maitland. Bryan has written several books on military uniforms and illustrated over 30 others, and is a regular contributor of articles and paintings to many magazines, including *Military Modelling* and *Military Illustrated*. With his brother Donald, he produced a monumental work on the development of British military uniforms – *The Thin Red Line* – published by Windrow and Greene in 1989. Bryan has been involved with the British Model Soldier Society since 1948, and for over 25 years was a committee member and an early recipient of the Society Fellowship. He has written numerous articles on the techniques of military modelling under the pseudonym, Stan Catchpol. Bryan Fosten's work is in great demand; his paintings are highly regarded by private collectors throughout the world, and by British Regimental Museums.

George and Christopher Newark,
Gidea Park, Essex, 1993

DEDICATED
to all "Tommies" past, present and future

ACKNOWLEDGEMENTS

We would like to thank the following people and organizations for their help and encouragement in producing this book. Firstly the Newark clan – Peter Newark, the writer; Derek Newark, the actor; Timothy Newark, the author, and Quentin Newark, the graphic designer. Jack and Doreen Jackson for their encouragement; I. C. Small of the Commonwealth War Graves Commission; W. Y. Carman; Major Margaret Easy, R.A.C.D.; Glenn Thompson of Dublin, and David Pennington of Pennington Designs for his expertise and invaluable advice. Finally, we thank Bryan Fosten for producing the magnificent paintings, the mainstay of this book, and for the help and advice he and his brother Don Fosten gave so readily, and for their friendship over the past 44 years.

11

Rudyard Kipling (1865 – 1936)
By Sir Philip Burne-Jones
Courtesy National Portrait Gallery

TOMMY

I went into a public-'ouse to get a pint o' beer,
The publican 'e up an' sez, "We serve no red-coats
    here."
The girls be'ind the bar they laughed an' giggled fit
    to die,
I outs into the street again an' to myself sez I:
        O it's Tommy this, an Tommy that, an'
            "Tommy, go away";
        But it's "Thank you, Mister Atkins," when
            the band begins to play,
        The band begins to play, my boys, the band
            begins to play,
        O it's "Thank you, Mister Atkins," when the
            band begins to play.

I went into a theatre as sober as could be,
They gave a drunk civilian room, but 'adn't none
    for me;
They sent me to the gallery or round the music-'alls,
But when it comes to fightin', Lord! they'll shove
    me in the stalls!
        For it's Tommy this, an' Tommy that, an'
            "Tommy, wait outside";
        But it's "Special train for Atkins" when the
            trooper's on the tide,
        The troopship's on the tide, my boys, the
            troopship's on the tide,
        O it's "Special train for Atkins" when the
            trooper's on the tide.

Yes, makin' mock o' uniforms that guard you while
     you sleep
Is cheaper than them uniforms, an' they're starva-
     tion cheap;
An' hustlin' drunken soldiers when they're goin'
     large a bit
Is five times better business than paradin' in full kit.
          Then it's Tommy this, an' Tommy that, an'
               "Tommy, 'ow's yer soul?"
          But it's "Thin red line of 'eroes" when the
               drums begin to roll,
          The drums begin to roll, my boys, the drums
               begin to roll,
          O it's "Thin red line of 'eroes" when the
               drums begin to roll.

We aren't no thin red 'eroes, nor we aren't no
     black-guards too,
But single men in barricks, most remarkable like
     you;
An' if sometimes our conduck isn't all your fancy
     paints,
Why, single men in barricks don't grow into plaster
     saints;
          While it's Tommy this, an' Tommy that, an'
               "Tommy, fall be'ind,"
          But it's "Please to walk in front, sir," when
               there's trouble in the wind,
          There's trouble in the wind, my boys, there's
               trouble in the wind,
          O it's "Please to walk in front, sir," when
               there's trouble in the wind.

TOMMY
Private – The Royal Sussex Regiment, 1890

You talk o' better food for us, an' schools, an' fires,
   an' all:
We'll wait for extry rations if you treat us rational.
Don't mess about the cook-room slops, but prove it
   to our face
The Widow's Uniform is not the soldier-man's dis-
   grace.
   For it's Tommy this, an' Tommy that, an'
      "Chuck him out, the brute!"
   But it's "Saviour of 'is country" when the
      guns begin to shoot;
   An' it's Tommy this, an' Tommy that, an'
      anything you please;
   An' Tommy ain't a bloomin' fool—you bet
      that Tommy sees!

"...single men in barricks..."

GUNGA DIN

You may talk o' gin and beer
When you're quartered safe out 'ere,
An' you're sent to penny-fights an' Aldershot it;
But when it comes to slaughter
You will do your work on water,
An' you'll lick the bloomin' boots of 'im that's got it.
Now in Injia's sunny clime,
Where I used to spend my time
A-servin' of 'Er Majesty the Queen,
Of all them blackfaced crew
The finest man I knew
Was our regimental bhisti, Gunga Din.
   He was "Din! Din! Din!
  "You limpin' lump o' brick-dust, Gunga Din!
   "Hi! slippery *hitherao*!
   "Water, get it ! *Panee lao*![1]
  "You squidgy-nosed old idol, Gunga Din."

The uniform 'e wore
Was nothin' much before,
An' rather less than 'arf o' that be'ind,
For a piece o' twisty rag
An' a goatskin water-bag
Was all the field-equipment 'e could find.
When the sweatin' troop-train lay
In a sidin' through the day,
Where the 'eat would make your bloomin' eyebrows
 crawl,
We shouted 'Harry By!'[2]
Till our throats were bricky-dry,
Then we wopped 'im 'cause 'e couldn't serve us all.
   It was "Din! Din! Din!
  "You 'eathen, where the mischief 'ave you been?
   "You put some *juldee*[3] in it'
   "Or I'll *marrow*[3] you this minute
  "If you don't fill up my helmet, Gunga Din!"

---

[1] Bring water swiftly
[2] Mr. Atkins equivalent for 'O brother.'
[3] Be Quick
[3] Hit you

17

'E would dot an' carry one
Till the longest day was done;
An' 'e didn't seem to know the use o' fear.
If we charged or broke or cut,
You could bet your bloomin' nut,
'E'd be waitin' fifty paces right flank rear.
With 'is mussick[1] on 'is back,
'E would skip with our attack,
An' watch us till the bugles made 'Retire,'
An' for all 'is dirty 'ide
'E was white, clear white, inside
When 'e went to tend the wounded under fire!
    It was "Din! Din! Din!"
    With the bullets kickin' dust-spots on the green.
      When the cartridges ran out,
      You could hear the front-files shout,
    "Hi! ammunition-mules an' Gunga Din!"

I sha'n't forgit the night
When I dropped be'ind the fight
With a bullet where my belt-plate should 'a' been.
I was chokin' mad with thirst,
An' the man that spied me first
Was our good old grinnin', gruntin' Gunga Din.
'E lifted up my 'ead,
An' he plugged me where I bled,
An' 'e guv me 'arf-a-pint o' water-green:
It was crawlin' and it stunk,
But of all the drinks I've drunk,
I'm gratefullest to one from Gunga Din.
    It was "Din! Din! Din!
    "'Ere's a beggar with a bullet through 'is spleen;
      "'E's chawin' up the ground,
      "An' 'e's kickin' all around:
    "For Gawd's sake git the water, Gunga Din!"

[1] Water-skin

Gunga Din
Private – 66th (Berkshire) Regiment, Afghanistan, 1880

'E carried me away
To where a dooli lay,
An' a bullet come an' drilled the beggar clean.
'E put me safe inside,
An' just before 'e died,
"I 'ope you liked your drink," sez Gunga Din.
So I'll meet 'im later on
At the place where 'e is gone—
Where it's always double drill and no canteen;
'E'll be squattin' on the coals
Givin' drink to poor damned souls,
An' I'll get a swig in hell from Gunga Din!
        Yes, Din! Din! Din!
    You Lazarushian-leather Gunga Din!
        Though I've belted you and flayed you,
        By the livin' Gawd that made you,
    You're a better man than I am, Gunga Din!

Regimental bhisties

MANDALAY

By the old Moulmein Pagoda, lookin' eastward to
    the sea,
There's a Burma girl a-settin', and I know she
    thinks o' me;
For the wind is in the palm-trees, and the temple-
    bells they say:
"Come you back, you British soldier; come you back
    to Mandalay!"
        Come you back to Mandalay,
        Where the old Flotilla lay:
        Can't you 'ear their paddles chunkin' from
            Rangoon to Mandalay?
        On the road to Mandalay,
        Where the flyin'-fishes play,
        An' the dawn comes up like thunder outer
            China 'crost the Bay!

'Er petticoat was yaller an' 'er little cap was green,
An' 'er name was Supi-yaw-lat—jes' the same as
    Theebaw's Queen,
An' I seed her first a-smokin' of a whackin' white
    cheroot,
An' a-wastin' Christian kisses on an 'eathen idol's
    foot:
        Bloomin' idol made o' mud—
        Wot they called the Great Gawd Budd—
        Plucky lot she cared for idols when I kissed
            'er where she stud!
        On the road to Mandalay...

When the mist was on the rice-fields an' the sun was
    droppin' slow,
She'd git 'er little banjo an' she'd sing *'Kulla-lo-lo!'*
With 'er arm upon my shoulder an' 'er cheek agin
    my cheek
We useter watch the steamers an' the *hathis* pilin'
    teak.
Elephints a-pilin' teak
In the sludgy, squdgy creek,
Where the silence 'ung that 'eavy you was 'arf afraid
    to speak!
On the road to Mandalay...

But that's all shove be'ind me—long ago an' fur
    away,
An' there ain't no 'buses runnin' from the Bank to
    Mandalay;
An' I'm learnin' 'ere in London what the ten-year
    soldier tells:
"If you've 'eard the East a-callin', you won't never
    'eed naught else."
No! you won't 'eed nothin' else
But them spicy garlic smells,
An' the sunshine an' the palm-trees an' the tinkly
    temple-bells;
On the road to Mandalay...

I am sick o' wastin' leather on these gritty pavin'
    stones,
An' the blasted Henglish drizzle wakes the fever in
    my bones;
Tho' I walks with fifty 'ousemaids outer Chelsea to
    the Strand,
An' they talks a lot o' lovin', but wot do they under-
    stand?
Beefy face an' grubby 'and—
Law! wot do they understand?
I've a neater, sweeter maiden in a cleaner, greener
    land!
On the road to Mandalay...

Mandalay
Corporal – Queen's (Royal West Surrey) Regiment, Burma, 1887

Ship me somewheres east of Suez, where the best is
    like the worst,
Where there aren't no Ten Commandments an' a
    man can raise a thirst;
For the temple-bells are callin', an' it's there that I
    would be—
By the old Moulmein Pagoda, looking lazy at the
    sea;
        On the road to Mandalay,
        Where the old Flotilla lay,
        With our sick beneath the awnings when we
            went to Mandalay!
        O the road to Mandalay,
        Where the flyin'-fishes play,
        An' the dawn comes up like thunder outer
            China 'crost the Bay!

British troops fording a
river in Burma, 1886

"FUZZY-WUZZY"

(SOUDAN EXPEDITIONARY FORCE)

We've fought with many men acrost the seas,
An' some of 'em was brave an' some was not:
The Paythan an' the Zulu an' Burmese;
But the Fuzzy was the finest o' the lot.
We never got a ha'porth's change of 'im:
'E squatted in the scrub an' 'ocked our 'orses,
'E cut our sentries up at Sua*kim*,
An' 'e played the cat an' banjo with our forces.
> So 'ere's *to* you, Fuzzy-Wuzzy, at your 'ome in
> the Soudan;
> You're a pore benighted 'eathen but a first-
> class fightin' man;
> We gives you your certificate, an' if you want
> it signed
> We'll come an' 'ave a romp with you when-
> ever you're inclined.

We took our chanst among the Kyber 'ills,
The Boers knocked us silly at a mile,
The Burman give us Irriwaddy chills,
An' a Zulu *impi* dished us up in style:
But all we ever got from such as they
Was pop to what the Fuzzy made us swaller;
We 'eld our bloomin' own, the papers say,
But man for man the Fuzzy knocked us 'oller.
> Then 'ere's *to* you, Fuzzy-Wuzzy, an' the mis-
> sis and the kid;
> Our orders was to break you, an' of course
> we went an' did.
> We sloshed you with Martinis, an' it wasn't
> 'ardly fair;
> But for all the odds agin' you, Fuzzy-Wuz, you
> broke the square.

'E 'asn't got no papers of 'is own,
'E 'asn't got no medals nor rewards,
So *we* must certify the skill 'e's shown
In usin' of 'is long two-'anded swords:
When 'e's 'oppin' in an' out among the bush
With 'is coffin-'eaded shield an' shovel-spear,
An 'appy day with Fuzzy on the rush
Will last an 'ealthy Tommy for a year.
      So 'ere's *to* you, Fuzzy-Wuzzy, an' your
          friends which are no more,
      If we 'adn't lost some messmates we would
          'elp you to deplore;
      But give an' take's the gospel, an' we'll call
          the bargain fair,
      For if you 'ave lost more than us, you crum-
          pled up the square!

'E rushes at the smoke when we let drive,
An', before we know, 'e's 'ackin' at our 'ead;
'E's all 'ot sand an' ginger when alive,
An' 'e's generally shammin' when 'e's dead.
'E's a daisy, 'e's a ducky, 'e's a lamb!
'E's a injia-rubber idiot on the spree,
'E's the on'y thing that doesn't give a damn
For a Regiment o' British Infantree!
      So 'ere's *to* you, Fuzzy-Wuzzy, at your 'ome in
          the Soudan;
      You're a pore benighted 'eathen but a first-
          class fightin' man;
      An' 'ere's *to* you, Fuzzy-Wuzzy, with your
          'ayrick 'ead of 'air—
      You big black boundin' beggar—for you
          broke a British square!

"Fuzzy-Wuzzy"
Private – 2nd Battalion, The Essex Regiment
(Mounted Infantry Camel Regiment), Sudan, 1885

Quarter Guard: 17th Lancers
(Duke of Cambridge's Own) 1896

Rough Riders, 1st Life Guards, 1880's

28

GENTLEMEN-RANKERS

To the legion of the lost ones, to the cohort of the
  damned
To my brethren in their sorrow overseas,
Sings a gentleman of England cleanly bred,
  machinely crammed,
And a trooper of the Empress, if you please.
Yes, a trooper of the forces who has run his own six
  horses,
And faith he went the pace and went it blind,
And the world was more than kin while he held the
  ready tin,
But to-day the Sergeant's something less than kind.
        We're poor little lambs who've lost our way,
            Baa! Baa! Baa!
        We're little black sheep who've gone astray,
            Baa—aa—aa!
        Gentlemen-rankers out on the spree,
        Damned from here to Eternity,
        God ha' mercy on such as we,
            Baa! Yah! Bah!

Oh, it's sweet to sweat through stables, sweet to
  empty kitchen slops,
And it's sweet to hear the tales the troopers tell,
To dance with blowzy housemaids at the regimental
  hops
And thrash the cad who says you waltz too well.
Yes, it makes you cock-a-hoop to be 'Rider' to your
  troop,
And branded with a blasted worsted spur,
When you envy, O how keenly, one poor Tommy
  being cleanly
Who blacks your boots and sometimes calls you
  "Sir."

If the home we never write to, and the oaths we
    never keep,
And all we know most distant and most dear,
Across the snoring barrack-room return to break
    our sleep,
Can you blame us if we soak ourselves in beer?
When the drunken comrade mutters and the great
    guard-lantern gutters
And the horror of our fall is written plain,
Every secret, self-revealing on the aching white-
    washed ceiling,
Do you wonder that we drug ourselves from pain?

We have done with Hope and Honour, we are lost
    to Love and Truth,
We are dropping down the ladder rung by rung,
And the measure of our torment is the measure of
    our youth.
God help us, for we knew the worst too young!
Our shame is clean repentance for the crime that
    brought the sentence,
Our pride it is to know no spur of pride,
And the Curse of Reuben holds us till an alien turf
    enfolds us
And we die, and none can tell Them where we died.
        We're poor little lambs who've lost our way,
            Baa! Baa! Baa!
        We're little black sheep who've gone astray,
            Baa—aa—aa!
        Gentlemen-rankers out on the spree,
        Damned from here to Eternity,
        God ha' mercy on such as we,
            Baa! Yah! Bah!

Gentlemen-Rankers
Trooper – 12th (Prince of Wales's Royal) Lancers, 1890

"...Now all you recruities what's drafted today..."

Khyber tribesman, 1898

THE YOUNG BRITISH SOLDIER

When the 'arf-made recruity goes out to the East
'E acts like a babe an' 'e drinks like a beast,
An' 'e wonders because 'e is frequent deceased
    Ere 'e's fit for to serve as a soldier.
        Serve, serve, serve as a soldier,
        Serve, serve, serve as a soldier,
        Serve, serve, serve as a soldier,
        So-oldier *of* the Queen!

Now all you recruities what's drafted to-day,
You shut up your rag-box an' 'ark to my lay,
An' I'll sing you a soldier as far as I may:
    A soldier what's fit for a soldier.
        Fit, fit, fit for a soldier...

First mind you steer clear o' the grog-sellers' huts,
For they sell you Fixed Bay'nets that rots out your
    guts—
Ay, drink that 'ud eat the live steel from your
    butts—
An' it's bad for the young British Soldier.
    Bad, bad, bad for the soldier...

When the cholera comes—as it will past a doubt—
Keep out of the wet and don't go on the shout,
For the sickness gets in as the liquor dies out,
An' it crumples the young British soldier.
    Crum-, crum-, crumples the soldier...

But the worst o' your foes is the sun over'ead:
You *must* wear your 'elmet for all that is said:
If 'e finds you uncovered 'e'll knock you down
    dead,
An' you'll die like a fool of a soldier.
    Fool, fool, fool of a soldier...

If you're cast for fatigue by a sergeant unkind,
Don't grouse like a woman nor crack on nor blind;
Be handy and civil, and then you will find
That it's beer for the young British soldier.
    Beer, beer, beer for the soldier...

Now, if you must marry, take care she is old—
A troop-sergeant's widow's the nicest I'm told,
For beauty won't help if your rations is cold,
Nor love ain't enough for a soldier.
    'Nough, 'nough, 'nough for a soldier...

If the wife should go wrong with a comrade, be loth
To shoot when you catch 'em—you'll swing, on my
    oath!—
Make 'im take 'er and keep 'er: that's Hell for them
    both,
An' you're shut o' the curse of a soldier.
    Curse, curse, curse of a soldier...

When first under fire an' you're wishful to duck,
Don't look nor take 'eed at the man that is struck,
Be thankful you're livin', and trust to your luck
And march to your front like a soldier.
    Front, front, front like a soldier...

When 'arf of your bullets fly wide in the ditch,
Don't call your Martini a cross-eyed old bitch;
She's human as you are—you treat her as sich,
An' she'll fight for the young British soldier.
    Fight, fight, fight for the soldier...

When shakin' their bustles like ladies so fine,
The guns o' the enemy wheel into line,
Shoot low at the limbers an' don't mind the shine,
For noise never startles the soldier.
    Start-, start-, startles the soldier....

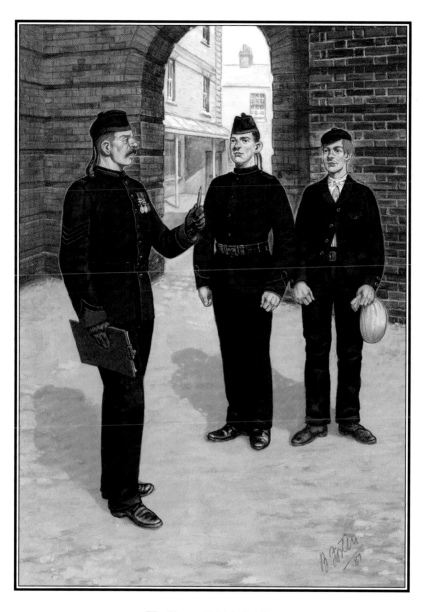

The Young British Soldier
Sergeant, Rifleman and recruit – King's Royal Rifle Corps, 1890

If your officer's dead and the sergeants look white,
Remember it's ruin to run from a fight:
So take open order, lie down, and sit tight,
And wait for supports like a soldier...
    Wait, wait, wait like a soldier ...

When you're wounded and left on Afghanistan's
    plains,
And the women come out to cut up what remains,
Jest roll to your rifle and blow out your brains
    An' go to your Gawd like a soldier.
        Go, go, go like a soldier,
        Go, go, go like a soldier,
        Go, go, go like a soldier,
        So-oldier *of* the Queen!

Posting a Sentry, 1897

36

BELTS

There was a row in Silver Street that's near to
    Dublin Quay,
Between an Irish regiment an' English cavalree;
It started at Revelly an' it lasted on till dark:
The first man dropped at Harrison's, the last
    forninst the Park.
        For it was:—'Belts, belts, belts, an' that's one
           for you!'
        An' it was 'Belts, belts, belts, an' that's done-
           for you!'
        O buckle an' tongue
        Was the song that we sung
        From Harrison's down to the Park!

There was a row in Silver Street—the regiments was
    out,
They called us "Delhi Rebels," an' we answered
    "Threes about!"
That drew them like a hornet's nest—we met them
    good an' large,
The English at the double an' the Irish at the
    charge.
        Then it was:—'Belts...

There was a row in Silver Street—an' I was in it too;
We passed the time o' day, an' then the belts went
    whirraru!
I misremember what occurred, but subsequint the
    storm
A *Freeman's Journal Supplemint* was all my uniform.
        O it was:—'Belts...

There was a row in Silver Street—they sent the Polis
    there,
The English were too drunk to know, the Irish
    didn't care;
But when they grew impertinint we simultaneous
    rose,
Till half o' them was Liffey mud an' half was
    tatthered clo'es.
        For it was:—'Belts...

There was a row in Silver Street—it might ha' raged
    till now,
But some one drew his side-arm clear, an' nobody
    knew how;
'Twas Hogan took the point an' dropped; we saw
    the red blood run:
An' so we all was murderers that started out in fun.
        While it was:—'Belts...

There was a row in Silver Street—but that put down
    the shine,
Wid each man whisperin' to his next: "'Twas never
    work o' mine!'
We went away like beaten dogs, an' down the street
    we bore him,
The poor dumb corpse that couldn't tell the bhoys
    were sorry for him.
        When it was:—'Belts...

There was a row in Silver Street—it isn't over yet,
For half of us are under guard wid punishments to
    get;
'Tis all a merricle to me as in the Clink I lie:
There was a row in Silver Street—begod, I wonder
    why!
        But it was:—'Belts, belts, belts, an' that's one
            for you!'
        An' it was 'Belts, belts, belts, an' that's done-
            for you!'
        O buckle an' tongue
        Was the song that we sung
        From Harrison's down to the Park!

Belts
Trooper – 9th (Queen's Royal) Lancers, Private – Royal Munster Fusiliers,
Sergeant – Dublin Metropolitan Police, 1892

Sergeant, Mounted Infantry Company,
Gordon Highlanders, 1895

Crossing a river under
Boer gunfire, 1900

40

M.I.
(MOUNTED INFANTRY OF THE LINE)

I Wish my mother could see me now, with a fence-
    post under my arm,
And a knife and a spoon in my putties that I found on
    a Boer farm,
Atop of a sore-backed Argentine, with a thirst that
    you couldn't buy.
        I used to be in the Yorkshires once
        (Sussex, Lincolns, and Rifles once),
        Hampshires, Glosters, and Scottish once! (ad
        lib.)
        But now I am M.I.

That is what we are known as—that is the name you
    must call
If you want officers' servants, pickets an' 'orse-guards
    an' all—
Details for buryin'-parties, company-cooks or sup-
    ply—
Turn out the chronic Ikonas! Roll up the
        _____[1]M.I!

My 'ands are spotty with veldt-sores, my shirt is a but-
    ton an' frill,
An' the things I've used my bay'nit for would make a
    tinker ill!
An' I don't know whose dam' column I'm in, nor
    where we're trekkin' nor why.
        I've trekked from the Vaal to the Orange
        once—
        From the Vaal to the greasy Pongolo once—
        (Or else it was called the Zambesi once)—
        For now I am M.I.

[1] Number according to taste and service of audience

41

That is what we are known as—we are the push you
    require
For outposts all night under freezin', an' rear-guard
    all day under fire.
Anything 'ot or unwholesome? Anything dusty or
    dry?
Borrow a bunch of Ikonas!
        Trot out the_____M.I.!

Our Sergeant-Major's a subaltern, our Captain's a
    Fusilier—
Our Adjutant's 'late of Somebody's 'Orse,' an' a
    Melbourne auctioneer;
But you couldn't spot us at 'alf a mile from the
    crackest caval-ry.
        They used to talk about Lancers once,
        Hussars, Dragoons, an' Lancers once,
        'Elmets, pistols, an' carbines once,
        But now we are M.I.

That is what we are known as—we are the orphans
    they blame
For beggin' the loan of an 'ead-stall an' makin' a
    mount to the same:
        Can't even look at an 'orselines but some one
        goes bellerin' 'Hi!
''Ere comes a burglin' Ikona!'
        Footsack you_____M.I.!

We're trekkin' our twenty miles a day an' bein'
    loved by the Dutch,
But we don't hold on by the mane no more, nor
    lose our stirrups—much;
An' we scout with a senior man in charge where the
    'oly white flags fly.
        We used to think they were friendly once,
        Didn't take any precautions once
        (Once, my ducky, an' only once!)
        But now we are M.I.

M. I.
Private – Mounted Infantry, The Duke of Wellington's
(West Riding Regiment), 1902

That is what we are known as—we are the beggars
    that got
Three days 'to learn equitation,' an' six months o'
    bloomin' well trot!
Cow-guns, an' cattle, an' convoys—an' Mister De
    Wet on the fly—
We are the rollin' Ikonas! We are the_____M.I.!

The new fat regiments come from home, imaginin'
    vain V.C.'s
(The same as our talky-fighty men which are often
    Number Threes[1]),
But our words o' command are "Scatter" an' "Close"
    an' "Let your wounded lie."
       We used to rescue 'em noble once,—
       Givin' the range as we raised 'em once,
       Gettin' 'em killed as we saved 'em once—
       But now we are M.I.

That is what we are known as—we are the lanterns
    you view
After a fight round the kopjes, lookin' for men that
    we knew;
Whistlin' an' callin' together, 'altin' to catch the
    reply:—
       ''Elp me! O 'elp me, Ikonas!"
       This way, the_____M.I.!

I wish my mother could see me now, a-gatherin'
    news on my own,
When I ride like a General up to the scrub and ride
    back like Tod Sloan,
Remarkable close to my 'orse's neck to let the shots
    go by.
       We used to fancy it risky once
       (Called it a reconnaissance once),
       Under the charge of an orf'cer once,
       But now we are M.I.

---

[1] Horse-holders when in action, and therefore generally under cover

That is what we are known as—that is the song you
must say
When you want men to be Mausered at one and a
penny a day;
We are no five-bob colonials—we are the 'ome-
made supply,
Ask for the London Ikonas!
Ring up the_____M.I.!

I wish myself could talk to myself as I left 'im a year
ago;
I could tell 'im a lot that would save 'im a lot on the
things that 'e ought to know!
When I think o' that ignorant barrack-bird, it
almost makes me cry.
I used to belong in an Army once
(Gawd! what a rum little Army once),
Red little, dead little Army once!
But now I am M.I.!

That is what we are known as—we are the men that
have been
Over a year at the business, smelt it an' felt it an'
seen.
We 'ave got 'old of the needful—you will be told by
and by;
Wait till you've 'eard the Ikonas, spoke to the old
M.I.!

Mount—march, Ikonas! Stand to your 'orses again!
Mop off the frost on the saddles, mop up the miles on the
plain.
Out go the stars in the dawnin', up goes our dust to the
sky,
Walk—trot, Ikonas! Trek jou,¹ the old M.I.!

¹ Get ahead.

45

Royal Artillery firing a salute at
The Tower of London, 1897

Royal Artillery in Action;
South Africa, 1900

46

UBIQUE

There is a word you often see, pronounce it as you
    may—
"You bike," "you bykwe," "ubbikwe"—alludin' to
    R.A.
It serves 'Orse, Field, an' Garrison as motto for a
    crest,
An' when you've found out all it means I'll tell you
    'alf the rest.

Ubique means the long-range Krupp be'ind the
    low-range 'ill—
Ubique means you'll pick it up an' while you do
    stand still.
Ubique means you've caught the flash an' timed it
    by the sound.
Ubique means five gunners' 'ash before you've
    loosed a round.

Ubique means Blue Fuse, an' make the 'ole to sink
    the trail.
Ubique means stand up an' take the Mauser's 'alf
    mile 'ail.
Ubique means the crazy team not God nor man can
    'old .
Ubique means that 'orse's scream which turns your
    innards cold!

Ubique means "Bank, 'Olborn, Bank—a penny all
    the way"—
The soothin', jingle-bump-an'-clank from day to
    peaceful day.
Ubique means "They've caught De Wet, an' now we
    shan't be long."
Ubique means "I much regret, the beggar's goin'
    strong!"

Ubique means the tearin' drift where, breech-
blocks jammed with mud,
The khaki muzzles duck an' lift across the khaki-
flood.
Ubique means the dancing plain that changes rocks
to Boers.
Ubique means the mirage again an' shellin' all out-
doors.

Ubique means "Entrain at once for Grootdefeat-
fontein"!
Ubique means "Off-load your guns"—at midnight
in the rain!
Ubique means "More mounted men. Return all
guns to store."
Ubique means the R.A.M.R. Infantillery Corps!

Ubique means that warnin' grunt the perished
linesman knows,
When o'er 'is strung an' sufferin' front the shrapnel
sprays 'is foes;
An' as their firin' dies away the 'usky whisper runs
From lips that 'aven't drunk all day: "The Guns
Thank Gawd, the Guns!"

Extreme, depressed, point-blank or short, end-first
or any'ow,
From Colesberg Kop to Quagga's Poort—from
Ninety-Nine till now—
By what I've 'eard the others tell an' I in spots 'ave
seen,
There's nothin' this side 'Eaven or 'Ell Ubique
doesn't mean!

Ubique
Sergeant – Royal Artillery, Sergeant – Gordon Highlanders,
Corporal – Highland Light Infantry, 1903

Officers of The Suffolk Regiment,
Minden Day, 1895

The Battle of Minden,
August 1st 1759

50

"THE MEN THAT FOUGHT AT MINDEN"
A SONG OF INSTRUCTION

The men that fought at Minden, they was rookies in
    their time—
So was them that fought at Waterloo!
All the 'ole command, yuss, from Minden to
    Maiwand,
They was once dam' sweeps like you!

Then do not be discouraged, 'Eaven is your 'elper,
We'll learn you not to forget;
An' you mustn't swear an' curse, or you'll only catch it
    worse,
For we'll make you soldiers yet!

The men that fought at Minden, they 'ad stocks
    beneath their chins,
Six inch 'igh an' more;
But fatigue it was their pride, and they would not be
    denied
To clean the cook-'ouse floor.

The men that fought at Minden, they had anarchistic
    bombs
Served to 'em by name of 'and-grenades;
But they got it in the eye (same as you will by an' by)
When they clubbed their field-parades.

The men that fought at Minden, they 'ad buttons up
    an' down,
Two-an'-twenty dozen of 'em told;
But they didn't grouse an' shirk at an hour's extry
    work,
They kept 'em bright as gold.

The men that fought at Minden, they was armed
    with musketoons,
Also, they was drilled by 'alberdiers;
I don't know what they were, but the sergeants took
    good care
    They washed be'ind their ears.

The men that fought at Minden, they 'ad ever cash
    in 'and
    Which they did not bank nor save,
But spent it gay an' free on their betters—such as
    me—
    For the good advice I gave.

The men that fought at Minden, they was civil —
    yuss, they was—
Never didn't talk o' rights an' wrongs,
But they got it with the toe (same as you will get it—
    so!)—
    For interrupting songs.

The men that fought at Minden, they was several
    other things
    Which I don't remember clear;
But that's the reason why, now the six-year men are
    dry,
    The rooks will stand the beer!

Then do not be discouraged, 'Eaven is your 'elper,
We'll learn you not to forget;
An' you mustn't swear an' curse, or you'll only catch it
    worse,
And we'll make you soldiers yet!

Soldiers yet, if you've got it in you—
All for the sake of the Core;
Soldiers yet, if we 'ave to skin you—
Run an' get the beer, Johnny Raw—Johnny Raw!
Ho! run an' get the beer, Johnny Raw!

"The Men that Fought at Minden"
Colour Sergeant and Privates – The Suffolk Regiment, 1890

Royal Engineers bridging the River Liffey,
Curragh Camp, Ireland, 1896

Officer and Sapper
Royal Engineers

54

SAPPERS

When the Waters were dried an' the Earth did
    appear,
("It's all one," says the Sapper),
      The Lord He created the Engineer,
      Her Majesty's Royal Engineer,
      With the rank and pay of a Sapper!

When the Flood come along for an extra monsoon,
'Twas Noah constructed the first pontoon
      To the plans of Her Majesty's, etc.

But after fatigue in the wet an' the sun,
Old Noah got drunk, which he wouldn't ha' done
      If he'd trained with, etc.

When the Tower o' Babel had mixed up men's *bat* [1],
Some clever civilian was managing that,
      An' none of, etc.

When the Jews had a fight at the foot of a hill,
Young Joshua ordered the sun to stand still,
      For he was a Captain of Engineers, etc.

When the Children of Israel made bricks without straw,
They were learnin' the regular work of our Corps,
      The work of, etc.

For ever since then, if a war they would wage,
Behold us a-shinin' on history's page—
      First page for, etc.

[1] Talk

We lay down their sidings an' help 'em entrain,
An' we sweep up their mess through the bloomin'
    campaign,
        In the style of, etc.

They send us in front with a fuse an' a mine
To blow up the gates that are rushed by the Line,
        But bent by, etc.

They send us behind with a pick an' a spade,
To dig for the guns of a bullock-brigade
        Which has asked for, etc.

We work under escort in trousers and shirt,
An' the heathen they plug us tail-up in the dirt,
        Annoying, etc.

We blast out the rock an' we shovel the mud,
We make 'em good roads an'—they roll down the
    khud¹,
        Reporting, etc.

We make 'em their bridges, their wells, an' their
    huts,
An' the telegraph-wire the enemy cuts,
        An' it's blamed on, etc.

An' when we return, an' from war we would cease,
They grudge us adornin' the billets of peace,
        Which are kept for, etc.

We build 'em nice barracks—they swear they are
    bad,
That our Colonels are Methodist, married or mad,
        Insultin', etc.

¹ Hillside

Sappers
Sergeant and Sappers – The Royal Engineers, 1895

They haven't no manners nor gratitude too,
For the more that we help 'em, the less will they do,
But mock at, etc.

Now the Line's but a man with a gun in his hand,
An' Cavalry's only what horses can stand,
When helped by, etc.

Artillery moves by the leave o' the ground,
But we are the men that do something all round,
For we are, etc.

I have stated it plain, an' my argument's thus
("It's all one," says the Sapper),
There's only one Corps which is perfect—that's us;
An' they call us Her Majesty's Engineers,
Her Majesty's Royal Engineers,
With the rank and pay of a Sapper!

ROYAL ENGINEERS.

HISTORY AND TRADITIONS.

The British "Military Engineer" is first mentioned in the Domesday Book compiled shortly after the Norman Conquest, and until 1715 the Chief Engineer had charge of all engines of war—including guns. In 1716, however, a Royal Warrant established the Royal Artillery to superintend the "King's Guns and Ordnance," whilst the Engineers, as a separate Corps, undertook special charge of the "King's Works." A company of Soldier Artificers, raised at Gibraltar by Sir William Green in 1772, was the origin of the rank and file of the Corps. Every Sapper is an Artisan and receives Engineer Pay, in addition to Regimental Pay, regulated by his skill at his trade. The motto, "Ubique"—"Everywhere,"—best explains why the Royal Engineers have neither Colours nor Battle Honours. Both Officers and Men are trained at the School of Military Engineering, founded at Chatham by Sir Charles Pasley in 1812. Their work comprises fortress, field, survey, railway, telegraph, bridging and ballooning duties. Officers of the Corps were originally ineligible for military command, but in 1868, Sir John Burgoyne was created a Field Marshal, and since then many of the highest Army Commands have been held by Royal Engineer Officers. Finally, the importance and duties of the Corps constantly increase with the increased application of science to military operations.

"SNARLEYOW"

This 'appened in a battle to a batt'ry of the corps
Which is first among the women an' amazin' first in
war;
An' what the bloomin' battle was I don't remember
now,
But Two's off-lead 'e answered to the name o'
Snarleyow.

>   Down in the Infantry, nobody cares;
>   Down in the Cavalry, Colonel 'e swears;
>   But down in the lead with the wheel at the flog
>   Turns the the bold Bombardier to a little
>   whipped dog!

They was movin' into action, they was needed very
sore,
To learn a little schoolin' to a native army corps,
They 'ad nipped against an uphill, they was tuckin'
down the brow,
When a tricky, trundlin' roundshot give the knock to
Snarleyow.

They cut 'im loose an' left 'im—'e was almost tore in
two—
But he tried to follow after as a well-trained 'orse
should do;
'E went an' fouled the limber, an' the Driver's
Brother squeals:
"Pull up, pull up for *Snarleyow*—'is head's between 'is
'eels!"

The Driver 'umped 'is shoulder, for the wheels was
goin' round,
An' there ain't no "Stop, conductor!" when a batt'ry's
changin' ground;
Sez 'e: "I broke the beggar in, an' very sad I feels,
'But I couldn't pull up, not for *you*—your 'ead
between your 'eels!"

'E 'adn't 'ardly spoke the word, before a droppin'
    shell
A little right the batt'ry an' between the sections
    fell;
An' when the smoke 'ad cleared away, before the
    limber wheels,
There lay the Driver's Brother with 'is 'ead between
    'is 'eels.

Then sez the Driver's Brother, an' 'is words was very
    plain,
"For Gawd's own sake get over me, an' put me out
    o' pain."
They saw 'is wounds was mortal, an' they judged
    that it was best,
So they took an' drove the limber straight across 'is
    back an' chest.

'The Driver 'e give nothin' 'cept a little coughin'
    grunt,
But 'e swung 'is 'orses andsome when it came to
    'Action Front!'
An' if one wheel was juicy, you may lay your Monday
    head
'Twas juicier for the niggers when the case begun to
    spread.

The moril of this story, it is plainly to be seen:
You 'avn't got no families when servin' of the
    Queen-
You 'avn't got no brothers, fathers, sisters, wives, or
    sons—
If you want to win your battles take an' work your
    bloomin' guns!
        Down in the Infantry, nobody cares;
        Down in the Cavalry, Colonel 'e swears;
        But down in the lead with the wheel at the
            flog
        Turns the bold Bombardier to a little
            whipped dog!

"Snarleyow"
Lance-Bombardier – Royal Field Artillery, Chelsea
Pensioner, Gunner – Royal Horse Artillery, 1892

"...For 'er sentries we stand by
the sea an' the land..."

THE WIDOW AT WINDSOR

'Ave you 'eard o' the Widow at Windsor
    With a hairy gold crown on 'er 'ead ?
She 'as ships on the foam—she 'as millions at 'ome,
    An' she pays us poor beggars in red.
        (Ow, poor beggars in red!)
There's 'er nick on the cavalry 'orses,
    There's 'er mark on the medical stores—
An' 'er troopers you'll find with a fair wind be'ind
    That takes us to various wars.
        (Poor beggars!—barbarious wars!)
        Then 'ere's to the Widow at Windsor,
            An' 'ere's to the stores an' the guns,
        The men an' the 'orses what makes up
            the forces
        O' Missis Victorier's sons.
        (Poor beggars! Victorier's sons!)

Walk wide o' the Widow at Windsor,
    For 'alf o' Creation she owns:
We 'ave bought 'er the same with the sword an' the
    flame,
    An' we've salted it down with our bones.
        (Poor beggars!—it's blue with our bones!)
Hands off o' the sons o' the Widow,
    Hands off o' the goods in 'er shop,
For the Kings must come down an' the Emperors
    frown
    When the Widow at Windsor says "Stop"!
        (Poor beggars!—we're sent to say "Stop"!)
        Then 'ere's to the Lodge o' the Widow,
            From the Pole to the Tropics it runs—
        To the Lodge that we tile with the rank
            an' the file,
        An' open in form with the guns.
        (Poor beggars!—it's always they guns!)

We 'ave 'eard o' the Widow at Windsor,
    It's safest to let 'er alone:
For 'er sentries we stand by the sea an' the land
    Wherever the bugles are blown.
        (Poor beggars!—an' don't we get blown!)
Take 'old o' the Wings o' the Mornin',
    An' flop round the earth till you're dead;
But you won't get away from the tune that they play
    To the bloomin' old rag over'ead.
        (Poor beggars!—it's 'ot over'ead!)
            Then 'ere's to the sons o' the Widow,
                Wherever, 'owever they roam.
            'Ere's all they desire, an' if they require
                A speedy return to their 'ome.
            (Poor beggars!—they'll never see 'ome!)

64

The Widow at Windsor
Private – The Gloucestershire Regiment, 1895

British Officers,
The Queen's Own Corps of Guides, 1879

Indian Cavalrymen of The Guides, 1898

THE BALLAD OF EAST AND WEST

Oh, East is East, and West is West, and never the twain
 shall meet
Till Earth and Sky stand presently at God's great
 Judgment Seat;
But there is neither East nor West, Border, nor Breed, nor
 Birth,
When two strong men stand face to face, tho' they come
 from the ends of the earth!

Kamal is out with twenty men to raise the Border-
 side,
And he has lifted the Colonel's mare that is the
 Colonel's pride:
He has lifted her out of the stable-door between the
 dawn and the day,
And turned the calkins upon her feet, and ridden
 her far away.
Then up and spoke the Colonel's son that led a
 troop of the Guides:
"Is there never a man of all my men can say where
 Kamal hides?"
Then up and spoke Mahommed Khan, the son of
 the Ressaldar:
"If ye know the track of the morning-mist, ye know
 where his pickets are.
"At dusk he harries the Abazai—at dawn he is into
 Bonair,
"But he must go by Fort Bukloh to his own place to
 fare,
"So if ye gallop to Fort Bukloh as fast as a bird can
 fly
"By the favour of God ye may cut him off ere he win
 to the Tongue of Jagai.
"But if he be past the Tongue of Jagai, right swiftly
 turn ye then,
"For the length and the breadth of that grisly plain
 is sown with Kamals men.

"There is rock to the left, and rock to the right, and
    low lean thorn between,
"And ye may hear a breech-bolt snick where never a
    man is seen."
The Colonel's son has taken a horse, and a raw
    rough dun was he,
With the mouth of a bell and the heart of Hell and
    the head of the gallows-tree.
The Colonel's son to the Fort has won, they bid him
    stay to eat—
Who rides at the tail of a Border thief, he sits not
    long at his meat.
He's up and away from Fort Bukloh as fast as he can
    fly,
Till he was aware of his father's mare in the gut of
    the Tongue of Jagai,
Till he was aware of his father's mare with Kamal
    upon her back,
And when he could spy the white of her eye, he
    made the pistol crack.
He has fired once, he has fired twice, but the
    whistling ball went wide.
"Ye shoot like a soldier," Kamal said. "Show now if
    ye can ride."
It's up and over the Tongue of Jagai, as blown dust-
    devils go,
The dun he fled like a stag of ten, but the mare like
    a barren doe.
The dun he leaned against the bit and slugged his
    head above,
But the red mare played with the snaffle-bars, as a
    maiden plays with a glove.
There was rock to the left and rock to the right, and
    low lean thorn between,
And thrice he heard a breech-bolt snick tho' never
    a man was seen.
They have ridden the low moon out of the sky, their
    hoofs drum up the dawn,
The dun he went like a wounded bull, but the mare
    like a new-roused fawn.
The dun he fell at a water-course—in a woeful heap
    fell he,

The Ballad of East and West
Lieutenant – The Queen's Own Corps of Guides, 1890

And Kamal has turned the red mare back, and
    pulled the rider free.
He has knocked the pistol out of his hand—small
    room was there to strive,
"'Twas only by favour of mine," quoth he, "ye rode
    so long alive:
"There was not a rock for twenty mile, there was not
    a clump of tree,
"But covered a man of my own men with his rifle
    cocked on his knee.
"If I had raised my bridle-hand, as I have held it low,
"The little jackals that flee so fast were feasting all in
    a row:
"If I had bowed my head on my breast, as I have
    held it high,
"The kite that whistles above us now were gorged
    till she could not fly."
Lightly answered the Colonel's son: "Do good to
    bird and beast,
"But count who come for the broken meats before
    thou makest a feast.
"If there should follow a thousand swords to carry
    my bones away,
"Belike the price of a jackal's meal were more than
    a thief could pay.
"They will feed their horse on the standing crop,
    their men on the garnered grain,
"The thatch of the byres will serve their fires when
    all the cattle are slain.
"But if thou thinkest the price be fair,—thy
    brethren wait to sup,
"The hound is kin to the jackal-spawn,—howl, dog,
    and call them up!
"And if thou thinkest the price be high, in steer and
    gear and stack,
"Give me my father's mare again, and I'll fight my
    own way back!"
Kamal has gripped him by the hand and set him
    upon his feet.
"No talk shall be of dogs," said he, "when wolf and
    grey wolf meet.
"May I eat dirt if thou hast hurt of me in deed or breath;

"What dam of lances brought thee forth to jest at
the dawn with Death?"
Lightly answered the Colonel's son: "I hold by the
blood of my clan:
"Take up the mare for my father's gift—by God, she
has carried a man!"
The red mare ran to the Colonel's son, and nuzzled
against his breast;
"We be two strong men," said Kamal then, "but she
loveth the younger best.
"So she shall go with a lifter's dower, my turquoise-
studded rein,
"My broidered saddle and saddle-cloth, and silver
stirrups twain."
The Colonel's son a pistol drew and held it muzzle-
end,
"Ye have taken the one from a foe," said he; "will ye
take the mate from a friend?"
"A gift for a gift," said Kamal straight; "a limb for
the risk of a limb.
"Thy father has sent his son to me, I'll send my son
to him!"
With that he whistled his only son, that dropped
from a mountain-crest—
He trod the ling like a buck in spring, and he
looked like a lance in rest.
"Now here is thy master," Kamal said, "who leads a
troop of the Guides,
"And thou must ride at his left side as shield on
shoulder rides.
"Till Death or I cut loose the tie, at camp and board
and bed,
"Thy life is his—thy fate it is to guard him with thy
head.
"So, thou must eat the White Queen's meat, and all
her foes are thine,
"And thou must harry thy father's hold for the
peace of the Border-line,
"And thou must make a trooper tough and hack thy
way to power—
Belike they will raise thee to Ressaldar when I am
hanged in Peshawur."

They have looked each other between the eyes, and
    there they found no fault,
They have taken the Oath of the Brother-in-Blood
    on leavened bread and salt:
They have taken the Oath of the Brother-in-Blood
    on fire and fresh-cut sod,
On the hilt and the haft of the Khyber knife, and
    the Wondrous Names of God.
The Colonel's son he rides the mare and Kamal's
    boy the dun,
And two have come back to Fort Bukloh where
    there went forth but one.
And when they drew to the Quarter-Guard, full
    twenty swords flew clear—
There was not a man but carried his feud with the
    blood of the mountaineer.
"Ha' done! ha' done!" said the Colonel's son. "Put
    up the steel at your sides!
"Last night ye had struck at a Border thief—tonight
    'tis a man of the Guides!"

Oh, East is East, and West is West, and never the twain
    shall meet
Till Earth and Sky stand presently at God's great
    Judgment Seat;
But there is neither East nor West, Border, nor Breed, nor
    Birth,
When two strong men stand face to face, tho' they come
    from the ends of the earth!

TROOPIN'

(OUR ARMY IN THE EAST)

Troopin' troopin', troopin' to the sea:
'Ere's September come again—the six-year men are
    free.
O leave the dead be'ind us, for they cannot come
    away
To where the ship's a-coalin' up that takes us 'ome
    to-day.
      We're goin' 'ome, we're goin' 'ome,
        Our ship is at the shore,
      An' you must pack your 'aversack,
        For we won't come back no more.
      Ho, don't you grieve for me,
        My lovely Mary-Ann,
      For I'll marry you yit on a fourp'ny bit
        as a time-expired man.

The Malabar's in 'arbour with the Jumner at 'er tail,
An' the time-expired's waitin' of 'is orders for to sail.
Ho! the weary waitin' when on Khyber 'ills we lay,
But the time-expired's waitin' of 'is orders 'ome
    to-day.

They'll turn us out at Portsmouth wharf in cold an'
    wet an' rain,
All wearin' Injian cotton kit, but we will not com-
    plain;
They'll kill us of pneumonia—for that's their little
    way—
But damn the chills and fever, men, we're goin'
    'ome to-day!

Troopin', troopin', winter's round again!
See the new draf's pourin' in for the old campaign;
Ho, you poor recruities, but you've got to earn your
    pay—
What's the last from Lunnon, lads? We're goin'
    there to-day.

Troopin', troopin', give another cheer—
'Ere's to English women an' a quart of English beer.
The Colonel an' the regiment an' all who've got to
    stay,
Gawd's mercy strike 'em gentle—Whoop! we're
    goin' 'ome to-day.
        We're goin' 'ome, we're goin' 'ome,
            Our ship is at the shore,
        An' you must pack your 'aversack,
            For we won't come back no more.
        Ho, don't you grieve for me,
            My lovely Mary-Ann,
        For I'll marry you yit on a fourp'ny bit
            As a time-expired man.

Northumberland Fusiliers
"...My First and best loved Battalion..." Kipling.

Troopin'
Private – The Northumberland Fusiliers, 1894

The Dorsetshire Regiment under
canvas in India, 1897

CHOLERA CAMP

We've got the cholerer in camp—it's worse than
    forty fights;
We're dyin' in the wilderness the same as Isrulites;
It's before us, an' be'ind us, an' we cannot get away,
An' the doctor's just reported we've ten more to-
    day!

Oh, strike your camp an' go, the bugle's callin',
    The Rains are fallin'—
The dead are bushed an' stoned to keep 'em safe below;
The Band's a-doin' all she knows to cheer us;
The chaplain's gone and prayed to Gawd to 'ear us— To
    'ear us—
O Lord, for it's a-killin' of us so!

Since August, when it started, it's been stickin' to
    our tail,
Though they've 'ad us out by marches an' they've
    'ad us back by rail;
But it runs as fast as troop-trains, and we can not get
    away;
An' the sick-list to the Colonel makes ten more to-
    day.

There ain't no fun in women nor there ain't no bite
    to drink;
It's much too wet for shootin', we can only march
    and think;
An' at evenin', down the *nullahs*, we can 'ear the
    jackals say,
"Get up, you rotten beggars, you've ten more to-
    day!"

'Twould make a monkey cough to see our way o'
	doin' things—
Lieutenants takin' companies an' captains takin'
	wings,
An' Lances actin' Sergeants—eight file to obey—
For we've lots o' quick promotion on ten deaths a
	day!

Our Colonel's white an' twitterly—'e gets no sleep
	nor food,
But mucks about in 'orspital where nothing does no
	good.
'E sends us 'eaps o' comforts, all bought from 'is
	pay—
But there aren't much comfort 'andy on ten deaths
	a day.

Our Chaplain's got a banjo, an' a skinny mule 'e
	rides,
An' the stuff 'e says an' sings us, Lord, it makes us
	split our sides!
With 'is black coat-tails a-bobbin' to *Ta-ra-ra Boom-
	der-ay!*
'E's the proper kind o' padre for ten deaths a day.

An' Father Victor 'elps 'im with our Roman
	Catholicks—
He knows an 'eap of Irish songs an' rummy con-
	jurin' tricks;
An' the two they works together when it comes to
	play or pray;
So we keep the ball a-rollin' on ten deaths a day.

Cholera Camp
Private – The King's (Liverpool Regiment), Chaplain
1st Class, Army Chaplains' Department, 1890

We've got the cholerer in camp—we've got it 'ot an'
sweet;
It ain't no Christmas dinner, but it's 'elped an' we
must eat.
We've gone beyond the funkin', 'cause we've found
it doesn't pay,
An' we're rockin' round the Districk on ten deaths
a day!

Then strike your camp an' go, the Rains are fallin',
    The Bugle's callin'!
The dead are bushed an' stoned to keep 'em safe below!
An' them that do not like it they can lump it,
An' them that can not stand it they can jump it;
We've got to die somewhere—some way—some'ow—
We might as well begin to do it now!
Then, Number One, let down the tent-pole slow,
Knock out the pegs an' 'old the corners—so!
Fold in the flies, furl up the ropes, an' stow!
Oh, strike—oh, strike your camp an' go!
    (Gawd 'elp us!)

80

DANNY DEEVER

"What are the bugles blowin' for?" said Files-on-
    Parade.
"To turn you out, to turn you out," the Colour-
    Sergeant said.
"What makes you look so white, so white?" said
    Files-on-Parade.
"I'm dreadin' what I've got to watch," the Colour-
    Sergeant said.
For they're hangin' Danny Deever, you can hear the
    Dead March play,
The regiment's in 'ollow square—they're hangin'
    him to-day;
They've taken of his buttons off an' cut his stripes
    away,
An' they're hangin' Danny Deever in the mornin'.

"What makes the rear-rank breathe so 'ard ? " said
    Files-on-Parade.
"It's bitter cold, it's bitter cold," the Colour-
    Sergeant said.
"What makes that front-rank man fall down?" says
    Files-on-Parade.
"A touch o' sun, a touch o' sun," the Colour-
    Sergeant said.
They are hangin' Danny Deever, they are marchin'
    of 'im round,
They 'ave 'alted Danny Deever by 'is coffin on the
    ground;
An' 'e'll swing in 'arf a minute for a sneakin'
    shootin' hound—
O they're hangin' Danny Deever in the mornin'!

"'Is cot was right-'and cot to mine," said Files-on-
    Parade.
"'E's sleepin' out an' far to night," the Colour-
    Sergeant said.
"I've drunk 'is beer a score o' times," said Files-on-
    Parade.
"'E's drinkin' bitter beer alone," the Colour-
    Sergeant said.
They are hangin' Danny Deever, you must mark
    'im to 'is place,
For 'e shot a comrade sleepin'—you must look 'im
    in the face;
Nine 'undred of 'is county an' the regiment's dis-
    grace,
While they're hangin' Danny Deever in the
    mornin'.

"What's that so black agin the sun?" said Files-on-
    Parade.
"It's Danny fightin' 'ard for life," the Colour-
    Sergeant said.
"What's that that whimpers over'ead?" said Files-on-
    Parade.
"It's Danny's soul that's passin' now," the Colour
    Sergeant said.
For they're done with Danny Deever, you can 'ear
    the quickstep play,
The regiment's in column, an' they're marchin' us
    away;
Ho! the young recruits are shakin', an' they'll want
    their beer to-day,
After hangin' Danny Deever in the mornin'.

82

Danny Deever
Colour Sergeant and Riflemen – The Rifle Brigade, 1894

The 39th Regiment at the Battle of Plassey,
23rd June, 1757

Cap badge of the Dorsetshire Regiment

84

ROUTE MARCHIN'

We're marchin' on relief over Injia's sunny plains,
A little front o' Christmas-time an' just be'ind the
    Rains;
Ho! get away you bullock-man, you've 'eard the
    bugle blowed,
There's a regiment a-comin' down the Grand
    Trunk Road;
        With its best foot first
        And the road a-sliding past,
        An' every bloomin' campin'-ground exactly
            like the last;
        While the Big Drum says,
        With 'is *"rowdy-dowdy-dow!"*—
        "Kiko kissywarsti don't you *hamsher argy jow?"*

Oh, there's them Injian temples to admire when
    you see,
There's the peacock round the corner an' the mon-
    key up the tree,
An' there's that rummy silver grass a-wavin' in the
    wind,
An' the old Grand Trunk a-trailin' like a rifle sling
    be'ind.
While it's best foot first,...

At half-past five's Revelly, an' our tents they down
    must come,
Like a lot of button mushrooms when you pick 'em
    up at 'ome.
But it's over in a minute, an' at six the column
    starts,
While the women and the kiddies sit an' shiver in
    the carts.
        An' it's best foot first,...

[1] Why don't you get on?

Oh, then it's open order, an' we lights our pipes an'
    sings,
An' we talks about our rations an' a lot of other
    things,
An' we thinks o' friends in England, an' we wonders
    what they're at,
An' 'ow they would admire for to hear us sling the
    bat.[1]
        An' it's best foot first,...

It's none so bad o' Sunday, when you're lyin' at
    your ease,
To watch the kites a-wheelin' round them feather-
    'eaded trees,
For although there ain't no women, yet there ain't
    no barrick-yards,
So the orficers goes shootin' an' the men they plays
    at cards
        Till it's best foot first,...

So 'ark an' 'eed, you rookies, which is always grum-
    blin' sore,
There's worser things than marchin' from Umballa
    to Cawnpore;
An' if your 'eels are blistered an' they feels to 'urt
    like' 'ell,
You drop some tallow in your socks an' that will
    make 'em well
        For it's best foot first,...

[1]   Language. Thomas's first and firmest conviction is that he is a
      profound Orientalist and a fluent speaker of Hindustani. As a
      matter of fact, he depends largely on the sign language.

Route Marchin'
1st Battalion, The Dorsetshire Regiment, 1897

We're marchin' on relief over Injia's coral strand,
Eight 'undred fightin' Englishmen, the Colonel,
   and the Band;
Ho! get away you bullock-man, you've 'eard the
   bugle blowed,
There's a regiment a-comin' down the Grand
   Trunk Road;
      With its best foot first
      And the road a-sliding past,
      An' every bloomin' campin'-ground exactly
         like the last;
      While the Big Drum says,
      With 'is "*rowdy,dowdy-dow!*"-
      "*Kiko kissywarsti* don't you *hamsher argy jow?*"

The 92nd Highlanders storming Gundi Mullah Sahibdad,
Kandahar, During the 2nd Afghan War, 1880

THE 'EATHEN

The 'eathen in 'is blindness bows down to wood an'
stone;
'E don't obey no orders unless they is 'is own;
'E keeps 'is side-arms awful: 'e leaves 'em all about,
An' then comes up the regiment an' pokes the
'eathen out.

All along o' dirtiness, all along o' mess,
All along o' doin' things rather-more-or-less,
All along of abby-nay,[1] kul,[2] an' hazar-ho,[3]
Mind you keep your rifle an' yourself jus' so!

The young recruit is 'aughty—'e draf's from Gawd
    knows where;
They bid 'im show 'is stockin's an' lay 'is mattress
    square;
'E calls it bloomin' nonsense—'e doesn't know, no
    more—
An' then up comes 'is Company an' kicks 'im round
    the floor!

The young recruit is 'ammered—'e takes it very
    'ard;
'E 'angs 'is 'ead an' mutters—'e sulks about the
    yard;
'E talks o' 'cruel tyrants' 'e'll swing for by-an'-by,
An' the others 'ears an' mocks 'im, an' the boy goes
    orf to cry.

[1] Not now,   [2] Tomorrow,   [3] Wait a bit

The young recruit is silly—'e thinks o' suicide;
'E's lost 'is gutter-devil; 'e 'asn't got 'is pride;
But day by day they kicks 'im, which 'elps 'im on a
    bit,
Till e' finds 'isself one mornin' with a full an' prop-
    er kit.

Gettin' clear o' dirtiness, gettin' done with mess,
Gettin' shut o' doin' things rather-more-or-less;
Not so fond of abby-nay, kul, nor hazar-ho,
Learns to keep 'is rifle an' 'isself jus' so!

The young recruit is 'appy—'e throws a chest to
    suit;
You see 'im grow mustaches; you 'ear 'im slap 'is
    boot;
'E learns to drop the 'bloodies' from every word 'e
    slings,
An' 'e shows an 'ealthy brisket when 'e strips for
    bars an' rings.

The cruel-tyrant-sergeants they watch 'im 'arf a year;
They watch 'im with 'is comrades, they watch 'im
    with 'is beer;
They watch 'im with the women at the regimental
    dance,
And the cruel-tyrant-sergeants send 'is name along
    for 'Lance.'

An' now 'e's 'arf o' nothin', an' all a private yet,
'Is room they up an' rags 'im to see what they will
    get;
They rags 'im low an' cunnin', each dirty trick they
    can,
But 'e learns to sweat 'is temper an' e' learns to
    sweat 'is man.

The 'Eathen
Guardsman and Drill Sergeant – Coldstream Guards, 1892

An', last, a Colour-Sergeant, as such to be obeyed,
'E schools 'is men at cricket, 'e tells 'em on parade;
They sees 'em quick an' 'andy, uncommon set an'
    smart,
An' so 'e talks to orficers which 'ave the Core at
    'eart.

'E learns to do 'is watchin' without it showin' plain;
'E learns to save a dummy, an' shove 'im straight
    again;
'E learns to check a ranker that's buyin' leave to
    shirk;
An' 'e learns to make men like 'im so they'll learn
    to like their work.

An' when it comes to marchin' he'll see their socks
    are right,
An' when it comes to action 'e shows 'em 'ow to
    sight;
'E knows their ways of thinkin' and just what's in
    their mind;
'E knows when they are takin' on an' when they 've
    fell be'ind.

'E knows each talkin' corpril that leads a squad
    astray;
'E feels 'is innards 'eavin', 'is bowels givin' way;
'E sees the blue-white faces all tryin' 'ard to grin,
An' 'e stands an' waits an' suffers till it's time to cap
    'em in.

An' now the hugly bullets come peckin' through
    the dust,
An' no one wants to face 'em, but every beggar
    must;
So, like a man in irons which isn't glad to go,
They moves 'em off by companies uncommon stiff
    an' slow.

Of all 'is five years' schoolin' they don't remember
much
Excep' the not retreatin', the step an' keepin'
touch.
It looks like teachin' wasted when they duck an'
spread an' 'op,
But if 'e 'adn't learned 'em they'd be all about the
shop!

An' now it's "'Oo goes backward?" an' now it's "'Oo
comes on?"
And now it's "Get the doolies," an' now the captain's gone;
An' now it's bloody murder, but all the while they
'ear
'Is voice, the same as barrick drill, a-shepherdin' the
rear.

'E's just as sick as they are, 'is 'eart is like to split,
But 'e works 'em, works 'em, works 'em till he feels
'em take the bit;
The rest is 'oldin' steady till the watchful bugles
play,
An' 'e lifts 'em, lifts 'em, lifts 'em through the
charge that wins the day!

The 'eathen in 'is blindness bows down to wood an' stone;
'E don't obey no orders unless they is 'is own;
The 'eathen in 'is blindness must end where 'e began .
But the backbone of the Army is the Non-commissioned
man!

Keep away from dirtiness—keep away from mess.
Don't get into doin' things rather-more-or-less!
Let's ha' done with abby-nay, kul, an' hazar-ho;
Mind you keep your rifle an yourself jus' so!

Sergeant – 11th Hussars (Prince Albert's Own)

"FOLLOW ME 'OME"

There was no one like 'im, 'Orse or Foot,
Nor any o' the Guns I knew;
An' because it was so, why, o' course 'e went an'
    died,
Which is just what the best men do.

> *So it's knock out your pipes an' follow me!*
> *An' it's, finish up your swipes an' follow me!*
> *Oh, 'ark to the big drum callin',*
>   *Follow me—follow me 'ome!*

'Is mare she neighs the 'ole day long,
She paws the 'ole night through,
An' she won't take 'er feed 'cause o' waitin' for 'is
    step,
Which is just what a beast would do.

'Is girl she goes with a bombardier
Before 'er month is through;
An' the banns are up in church, for she's got the
    beggar hooked,
Which is just what a girl would do.

We fought 'bout a dog—last week it were—
No more than a round or two;
But I strook 'im cruel 'ard, an' I wish I 'adn't now,
Which is just what a man can't do.

'E was all that I 'ad in the way of a friend,
An' I've 'ad to find one new;
But I'd give my pay an' stripe for to get the beggar
    back,
Which it's just too late to do.

So it's knock out your pipes an' follow me!
An' it's finish off your swipes an follow me!
Oh,'ark to the fifes a-crawlin'!
    Follow me—follow me 'ome!

Take 'im away! 'E's gone where the best men go.
Take 'im away! An' the gun wheels turnin' slow.
Take 'im away! There's more from the place 'e
    come.
Take 'im away, with the limber an' the drum.

For it's "Three rounds blank" an' follow me,
An' it's "Thirteen rank" an' follow me;
 Oh, passin' the love o' women,
    Follow me—follow me 'ome!

A Military Funeral, 1897

"Follow Me 'Ome"
Trooper – 11th Hussars (Prince Albert's Own), 1890

A Mountain Battery on the march

"Screw-Guns" in action

SCREW-GUNS

Smokin' my pipe on the mountings, sniffin' the
    mornin' cool,
I walks in my old brown gaiters along o' my old
    brown mule,
With seventy gunners be'ind me, an' never a beggar
    forgets
It's only the pick of the Army that handles the dear
    little pets—'Tss! 'Tss!
        For you all love the screw-guns—the screw-
            guns they all love you!
        So when we call round with a few guns, o'
            course you will know what to do—hoo! hoo!
        Jest send in your Chief an' surrender—it's
            worse if you fights or you runs:
        You can go where you please, you can skid
            up the trees, but you don't get away from
            the guns!

They sends us along where the roads are, but mostly
    we goes where they ain't:
We'd climb up the side of a sign-board an' trust to
    the stick o' the paint:
We've chivied the Naga an' Looshai, we've give the
    Afreedeeman fits,
For we fancies ourselves at two thousand, we guns
    that are built in two bits—'Tss! 'Tss!
For you all love the screw-guns...

If a man doesn't work, why, we drills 'im an' teaches
    'im 'ow to behave;
If a beggar can't march, why, we kills 'im an' rattles
    'im into 'is grave.
You've got to stand up to our business an' spring
    without snatchin' or fuss.
D'you say that you sweat with the field-guns? By
    God, you must lather with us—'Tss! 'Tss!
For you all love the screw-guns...

The eagles is screamin' around us, the river's a-
    moanin' below,
We're clear o' the pine an' the oak-scrub, we're out
    on the rocks an' the snow,
An' the wind is as thin as a whip-lash what carries
    away to the plains
The rattle an' stamp o' the lead-mules—the jinglety
    jink o' the chains—'Tss! 'Tss!
For you all love the screw-guns...

There's a wheel on the Horns o' the Mornin', an' a
    wheel on the edge o' the Pit,
An' a drop into nothin' beneath you as straight as a
    beggar can spit:
With the sweat runnin' out o' your shirt-sleeves, an'
    the sun off the snow in your face,
An' 'arf o' the men on the drag-ropes to hold the
    old gun in 'er place—'Tss! 'Tss!
For you all love the screw-guns...

Smokin' my pipe on the mountings, sniffin' the
    mornin' cool,
I climbs in my old brown gaiters along o' my old
    brown mule.
The monkey can say what our road was – the wild-
    goat 'e knows where we passed.
Stand easy, you long-eared old darlin's! Out drag-
    ropes! With shrapnel! Hold fast—'Tss! 'Tss!

For you all love the screw-guns—the screw-guns they
    all love you!
So when we take tea with a few guns, o' course you
    will know what to do—hoo! hoo!
Jest send in your Chief an' surrender—it's worse if
    you fights or you runs:
You may hide in the caves, they'll be only your
    graves, but you can't get away from the guns!

Screw-Guns
Sergeant – Mountain Battery, Royal Artillery, 1897

Royal Marine Artillery
at gunnery practice, 1897

Types of the Royal Marine Light Light Infantry, 1890's

"SOLDIER AN' SAILOR TOO"

As I was spittin' into the Ditch aboard o' the *Croco-dile*,
I seed a man on a man-o'-war got up in the Reg'lars'
    style.
'E was scrapin' the paint from off of 'er plates, an' I
    sez to 'im, "'Oo are you?"
Sez 'e, "I'm a Jolly—'Er Majesty's Jolly—soldier an'
    sailor too!"
Now 'is work begins by Gawd knows when, and 'is
    work is never through;
'E isn't one o' the reg'lar Line, nor 'e isn't one of
    the crew.
'E's a kind of a giddy harumfrodite—soldier an'
    sailor too!

An' after I met 'im all over the world, a-doin' all
    kinds of things,
Like landin' 'isself with a Gatlin' gun to talk to them
    'eathen kings;
'E sleeps in an 'ammick instead of a cot, an' 'e drills
    with the deck on a slew,
An' 'e sweats like a Jolly—'Er Majesty's Jolly—sol-
    dier an' sailor too!
For there isn't a job on the top o' the earth the beg-
    gar don't know, nor do—
You can leave 'im at night on a bald man's 'ead, to
    paddle 'is own canoe—
'E's a sort of a bloomin' cosmopolouse—soldier an'
    sailor too.

We've fought 'em in trooper, we've fought 'em in
    dock, and drunk with 'em in betweens,
When they called us the seasick scull'ry-maids, an
    we called 'em the Ass Marines;
But, when we was down for a double fatigue, from
    Woolwich to Bernardmyo,
We sent for the Jollies—'Er Majesty's Jollies—sol-
    dier an' sailor too!
They think for 'emselves, an' they steal for 'em-
    selves, and they never ask what's to do,
But they're camped an' fed an' they're up an' fed
    before our bugle's blew.
Ho! they ain't no limpin' procrastitutes—soldier an'
    sailor too.

You may say we are fond of an 'arness-cut, or 'ootin'
    in barrick-yards,
Or startin' a Board School mutiny along o' the
    Onion Guards;
But once in a while we can finish in style for the
    ends of the earth to view,
The same as the Jollies—'Er Majesty's Jollies— sol-
    dier an' sailor too!
They come of our lot, they was brothers to us; they
    was beggars we'd met an' knew;
Yes, barrin' an inch in the chest an' the arm, they
    was doubles o' me an' you;
For they weren't no special chrysanthemums— sol-
    dier an' sailor too!

"Soldier and Sailor Too"
Private – Royal Marine Light Infantry, 1890

To take your chance in the thick of a rush, with firing all about,
Is nothing so bad when you've cover to 'and, an'
   leave an' likin' to shout;
But to stand an' be still to the *Birken'ead* drill is a
   damn tough bullet to chew,
An' they done it, the Jollies—'Er Majesty's Jollies —
   soldier an' sailor too!
Their work was done when it 'adn't begun; they was
   younger nor me an' you;
Their choice it was plain between drownin' in 'eaps
   an' bein' mopped by the screw,
So they stood an' was still to the *Birken'ead* drill, soldier an' sailor too!

We're most of us liars, we're 'arf of us thieves, an'
   the rest are as rank as can be,
But once in a while we can finish in style (which I
   'ope it won't 'appen to me).
But it makes you think better o' you an' your
   friends, an' the work you may 'ave to do,
When you think o' the sinkin' *Victorier's* Jollies— sol-
   dier an' sailor too!
Now there isn't no room for to say ye don't know—
   they 'ave proved it plain and true—
That whether it's Widow, or whether it's ship,
   Victorier's work is to do,
An' they done it, the Jollies—'Er Majesty's Jollies —
   soldier an' sailor too!

THE IRISH GUARDS

We're not so old in the Army list,
    But we're not so young at our trade,
For we had the honour at Fontenoy
    Of meeting the Guards' Brigade.
'Twas Lally, Dillon, Bulkeley, Clare,
    And Lee that led us then,
And after a hundred and seventy years
    We're fighting for France again!
Old Days! The wild geese are flighting,
    Head to the storm as they faced it before!
For where there are Irish there's bound to be fighting,
    And when there's no fighting, it's Ireland no more!
        Ireland no more!

The fashion's all for khaki now,
    But once through France we went
Full-dressed in scarlet Army cloth,
    The English—left at Ghent.
They're fighting on our side to-day
    But, before they changed their clothes,
The half of Europe knew our fame,
    As all of Ireland knows!
Old Days! The wild geese are flying,
    Head to the storm as they faced it before!
For where there are Irish there's memory undying,
    And when we forget, it is Ireland no more!
        Ireland no more!

From Barry Wood to Gouzeaucourt,
    From Boyne to Pilkem Ridge,
The ancient days come back no more
    Than water under the bridge.
But the bridge it stands and the water runs as red as
    yesterday,
And the Irish move to the sound of the guns
    Like salmon to the sea.
Old Days! The wild geese are ranging,
    Head to the storm as they faced it before!
For where there are Irish their hearts are un-changing,
    And when they are changed, it is Ireland no more!
        Ireland no more!

We're not so old in the Army List,
    But we're not so new in the ring,
For we carried our packs with Marshal Saxe
    When Louis was our King.
But Douglas Haig's our Marshal now
    And we're King George's men,
And after one hundred and seventy years
    We're fighting for France again!
Ah, France! And did we stand by you,
When life was made splendid with gifts and rewards?
Ah, France! And will we deny you
    In the hour of your agony, Mother of Swords?
Old Days! The wild geese are flighting,
    Head to the storm as they faced it before!
For where there are Irish there's loving and fighting,
    And when we stop either, it's is Ireland no more!
        Ireland no more!

108

The Irish Guards
Guardsman – Irish Guards, Poilu – French Infantry, 1918

Gethsemane
An Unknown Soldier

GETHSEMANE

The Garden called Gethsemane
   In Picardy it was,
And there the people came to see
   The English soldiers pass.
We used to pass—we used to pass
   Or halt, as it might be,
And ship our masks in case of gas
   Beyond Gethsemane.

The Garden called Gethsemane,
   It held a pretty lass,
But all the time she talked to me
   I prayed my cup might pass.
The officer sat on the chair,
   The men lay on the grass,
And all the time we halted there
   I prayed my cup might pass.

It didn't pass—it didn't pass—
   It didn't pass from me.
I drank it when we met the gas
   Beyond Gethsemane!

"He is out on active service
Wiping something off the slate"

112

Notes on the Poems

Tommy, pages 13-16

Although the origin of the nickname 'Tommy' for a British soldier cannot be traced with any certainty, when a specimen army record book for soldiers was circulated by the War Office in 1815 the name entered as an example for unit paymasters to follow was Thomas Atkins, No. 6 Company, 1st Battalion, 23rd Regiment of Foot. The name has stuck as a sobriquet for the British soldier and, shortened to 'Tommy' is a name recognized the world over. In this poem Kipling chronicled the sardonic reaction of a private soldier to the way society treated him - despised and unwanted in peacetime, but cheered and feted in times of war.

Gunga Din , pages 17-20

The exploits of Gunga Din, the name given by Kipling to the character in this ballad, were based on the heroic actions of Juma, a water-carrier to The Guides at the siege of Delhi during the Great Mutiny of 1857. Kipling set *Gunga Din* in a later Victorian period and painted a graphic description of life in the British Army in India in the 1880's. The 66th (Berkshire) Regiment formed part of a field force commanded by General Burrows during the Second Afghan War which made a desperate last stand against overwhelming odds at Maiwand on 27th July, 1880. Out of a total strength of 488 men the Regiment suffered 308 casualties.

Mandalay, pages 21-24

During the Third Burmese War, 1885-91, a flotilla of river steamers towing barges, roofed over with canvas awnings, transported a 10,000-strong British army up the Irrawaddy to Mandalay to overthrow the tyrannical King Theebaw. Kipling briefly visited Burma in 1889 and actually *saw* an old Moulmein pagoda; *heard* the tinkly temple bells; *sniffed* the spicy air, and 'fell deeply and irrevocably in love' with a Burmese girl sitting on the steps of the pagoda. The same sights and sounds influenced many British soldiers and Kipling expressed the nostalgia they felt when back on mundane garrison duty in Britain – and so produced one of his best known poems.

113

Notes on the Poems

'Fuzzy-Wuzzy', pages 25-26

'Fuzzy-Wuzzy' was the name given to the Hadendowa Beja warriors of the Mahdi's army by British soldiers who fought them in the Sudan in 1881-85 and 1896-98. The Beja wore their hair frizzed out into a halo – hence the nickname. This poem records 'Tommy's' respect for their reckless bravery in rushing at the British squares armed only with swords and spears. The majority of 2nd Battalion, The Essex Regiment formed part of Wolseley's River Column which vainly sought to rescue General Gordon, besieged at Khartoum in 1884, by way of the Nile. Other Essex men served in the Mounted Infantry Camel Regiment attempting the relief overland.

Gentleman-Rankers, pages 29-30

Disgraced gentlemen, the proverbial 'black sheep' of the family, often joined the army as troopers in Victorian times to seek anonymity. Three 'gentleman-rankers' of the 9th Lancers serving in India, one an old schoolmate from United Services College days, called on Kipling at the *Gazette* offices in Lahore and may have provided the inspiration for this poem. Olders readers may recall Bing Crosby singing an American collegiate-style song with similar words such as '*gentlemen-songsters out on the spree*' with the strange title of *The Whiffenpoof Song*. Even older readers may remember Rudy Vallee singing the same song!

The Young British Soldier, pages 33-36

When this ballad was published in 1892 the bulk of recruits to the British Army came from the poor and disadvantaged elements of the population. Most of them joined to escape grinding poverty; a few for the glamour of the uniform, and some for the opportunity to travel. The army gave them a home, comradeship, pride in their regiment, and a fair chance of getting killed or dying from disease in some far flung corner of the British Empire. A high proportion were agricultural labourers, although Kipling described the East Surrey Regiment stationed in India as 'a London recruited confederacy of skilful dog-stealers, some of them my good and loyal friends'.

Notes on the Poems

Belts, pages 37-38

From the insults hurled at each other by the participants in this brawl in Dublin '...*Between an Irish regiment an' English cavalree ...*' we can hazard a guess at identifying the regiments involved as the Royal Munster Fusiliers and the 9th (Queen's Royal) Lancers. Both regiments served at Delhi during the Indian Mutiny and the unkind 'Delhi Rebels' taunt to the Munsters would refer to their previous service as Bengal European Fusiliers. 'Threes about', a quick retreat, would be meant as an insult to the 9th Lancers who gallantly earned the nickname 'Delhi Spearmen' during the Great Mutiny.

M.I., pages 41-45

Infantry battalions added Mounted Infantry companies to their strength in the 1880's to increase mobility. The hit-and-run tactics of Boer commandos during the South African War, 1899-1902, highlighted the need for large formations of mounted infantrymen in place of traditional cavalry regiments, so mounted infantry companies of line regiments were drawn together and formed into battalions. Unfortunately, they were not used to their full potential and many M.I. battalions served only as Divisional Troops leading Kipling to describe them as, among other things, '...*Details for burying parties, company cooks or supply...*'.

Ubique, pages 47-48

The title of this ballad is the motto of the Royal Regiment of Artillery and literally means - everywhere. It signifies that 'Gunners' have served in every campaign fought by the British Army since 1716. Kipling wrote *Ubique* shortly after the Boer War, 1899-1902; at that time the artillery arm comprised Royal Horse Artillery, Royal Field Artillery and Royal Garrison Artillery. In the painting illustrating this poem Bryan Fosten has shown a Royal Field Artillery sergeant addressing two Scottish NCO's at Edinburgh Castle in 1903. He is wearing the Brodrick cap, an unpopular and therefore short-lived, headress.

Notes on the Poems

'The Men That Fought at Minden', pages 51-52

The Suffolk Regiment was one of six British infantry regiments that routed a huge force of French cavalry at Minden, Germany, in August 1759, during the Seven Years War. On the way to Minden Heath, soldiers plucked roses from the hedgerows and wore them in their hats during the battle. From then on the Suffolks decorated their headdress with roses on the anniversary of the battle, a practice carried out to this day by the Royal Anglian Regiment. Rudyard Kipling nearly died from pneumonia on a visit to New York in 1899; upon his recovery telegrams of congratulations arrived from all over the world – including one from the Sergeants' Mess of the Suffolk Regiment.

Sappers, pages 55-58

A Staff Corps of engineer officers was established by the Board of Ordnance in 1716, and a Corps of Royal Military Artificers composed of NCO's and private tradesman was formed in 1787. The latter corps became the Royal Sapppers and Miners in 1813 and joined with the Engineer Corps in 1856 to form the Corps of Royal Engineers. Apart from military engineering such as building roads, bridges and barracks, Sappers pioneered the use of military aircraft before the formation of the Royal Flying Corps in 1912; experimented with tanks before the Tank Corps was formed in 1917, and were responsible for communications before the Royal Corps of Signals was created in 1920.

'Snarleyow', pages 59-60

This ballad was dramatized by Kipling from a passage in an autobiography by Staff-Sergeant N.W. Bancroft who served in the Bengal Horse Artillery from 1832 to 1866. Bancroft was a Bombardier at the Battle of Ferozeshah,December 1845, during the First Sikh War, and graphically described the incident of Snarleyow. His book was published in 1885 and Kipling reviewed it for the *Civil and Military Gazette.* It is thought Kipling partly based the character of Private Mulvaney of *Soldiers Three* on Sergeant Bancroft. The Chelsea Pensioner in Bryan Fosten's painting wears medals for the 1st Sikh War, 2nd Sikh War, and the Indian Mutiny.

Notes on the Poems

The Widow at Windsor, pages 63-64

The death of her husband Prince Albert in 1861 so devastated Queen Victoria that she withdrew from public life for many years. For the rest of her life she dressed in black and wore a white widow's cap and was often referred to as the 'Widow at Windsor'. It is said, without foundation, that this poem annoyed Queen Victoria and was the reason Kipling did not receive a royal accolade, when in fact he refused a KCB, KCMG, CH, OM, and the Poet Laureateship. Bryan Fosten's illustration shows a private of the Gloucestershire Regiment expounding his views about 'The Widder'; note the back badge on his glengarry.

The Ballad of East and West, pages 67-72

'...*the Colonel's son that led a troop of the Guides...*'would have been a member of the Queen's Own Corps of Guides raised in 1846 by Lieutenant Harry Lumsden. It consisted of a cavalry squadron and two infantry companies and is credited with being the first regiment to be clothed entirely in khaki uniforms. Apart from constantly policing the North-West Frontier of India, the Guides distinguished themselves in many campaigns gaining numerous Battle Honours, among them, Delhi 1857, Kabul 1879, Mesopotamia 1917-18 and North Africa 1940-43. It is still in existence as the Guides Cavalry (Frontier Force) Regiment of the Pakistan Army.

Troopin ' pages73-74

The *Malabar* and *Jumna* were two of the troopships transporting the army to and from India in Kipling's time. They could accommodate a full battalion of infantry with their families, albeit in cramped conditions below the waterline. The 2nd Battalion, Northumberland Fusiliers was stationed at Mian Mir Cantonment, Lahore, in the mid-1880's when Kipling was working for the *Civil and Military Gazette*. He dined with them quite often and described them as 'my first and best loved battalion' and the 'Tyneside Tail-twisters'. The minimum period for a soldier to serve was 6 years with the Colours; inverted chevrons were worn on the lower sleeve to denote varying years of service.

Notes on the Poems

Cholera Camp, pages 77-80

Cholera is an acute infectious disease transmitted by contaminated water or food, and is marked by severe diarrhoea, vomiting and agonizing cramps. It is endemic to India and many thousands of British soldiers succumbed to this sickness. A regiment hit by cholera would march out of garrison and set up 'cholera camps' in the countryside until the affliction ran its course. Chaplains have ministered not only to the spiritual needs of the British Army since 1662, but were invaluable in helping troops overcome the ravages of cholera and other infections. Four chaplains have been awarded the Victoria Cross.

Danny Deever, pages 81-82

A public military execution is the poignant subject of this poem. The condemned man's regiment would be formed into a hollow square, with the gallows in the centre, to witness the hanging. The convicted man might have been sentenced to death by court martial, most likely for killing a comrade. Kipling reported such executions for the *Civil and Military Gazette*, but a description by Lord Lucan (1845-1911) of a military execution he witnessed while serving with the Rifle Brigade in India in the 1880's is thought to have provided Kipling with the scenario for *Danny Deever*.

Route Marchin', pages 85-88

Primus in Indis was the unique motto of the Dorsetshire Regiment, proudly proclaiming to be 'First in India'. As the 39th Regiment of Foot it was the first King's regiment to land in India in 1754, and the only Crown infantry regiment under Clive at the Battle of Plassey in 1757. Later service in India gained them Battle Honours at Maharajpore 1843, and Tirah 1897. The Grand Trunk Road ran from Khyber to Calcutta and Kipling's inspirational lines '...*Eight 'undred fighting Englishmen, the Colonel, and the Band...*-' is reflected in Bryan Fosten's painting of the Dorsetshire Regiment on the march.

Notes on the Poems

The 'Eathen, pages 89-93

This poem charts the progress of a Victorian soldier from recruit to Colour-sergeant. From the sometimes brutal way of teaching a man to conform to army requirements; through promotion by merit, to leading his men in a successful skirmish. Our illustration shows a scene familiar to all soldiers - kit inspection. We have chosen the Coldstream Guards to represent this ballad as Kipling became familiar with the sight of Guardsmen at Gattis Music Hall and wrote – 'The Private soldier in India I thought I knew fairly well. His English brother (in the Guards mostly) sat and sang at my elbow any night I chose'.

"Follow me 'ome", pages 95-96

Comradeship in the British Army was a theme Kipling used many times in his writing. The title characters in *Soldiers Three*, Privates Ortheris, Mulvaney and Learoyd, epitomized this theme as they ran the gamut of emotions experienced by three men from different backgrounds brought together in the melting pot of the army. *Follow me 'ome* carried a similar pattern with friends fighting each other one minute, and defending each other the next. Kipling used a passage from the story of David and Jonathan in the Bible, 2 Samuel, Chapter 1: 26, to round off this poem – 'Thy love to me was wonderful, passing the love of women'.

Screw-guns, pages 99-100

'Screw-guns' were the small 2.5 inch rifled muzzle-loading guns used in India by Mountain Batteries of the Royal Artillery. The barrel was too heavy for one mule to carry, so it was made in two parts and screwed together with a junction nut to prepare for action. One mule carried the breech section; another the muzzle section; a third the gun carriage; a fourth had two wheels slung either side of the pack saddle, while other mules carried ammunition, tools and stores. The screw-gun was introduced in 1879; weighed 400lbs, and could project a 7lb shrapnel shell 3,300 yards.

Notes on the Poems

Soldier and Sailor Too, pages 103-106

The Royal Marines, 'The Jollies', have rendered valiant service on land and sea since 1664, and prior to 1923 comprised the Royal Marine Artillery and Royal Marine Light Infantry. The *Crocodile* was one of the troopships conveying the army to and from India in the latter half of the 19th century. The references to the *Birkenhead* and *Victoria* recall the famous shipwreck off Africa in 1852 (when troops safely saw the women and children into lifeboats then lined up on deck as the *Birkenhead* sank) and the collision of *HMS Victoria* and *HMS Camperdown* in 1893. Both incidents involved heavy loss of life among soldiers, sailors and marines.

The Irish Guards, pages 107-108

In this poem Kipling linked 'The Wild Geese', Irish mercenaries serving France in the 18th century, with the presence of the Irish Guards in France during The Great War, 1914-18. Sadly, his only son Lieutenant John Kipling, 2nd Battalion, Irish Guards was reported missing believed killed at the Battle of Loos in October, 1915. The Irish Guards served in France and Flanders with the Guards Division, gaining many Battle Honours, among them Mons, Aisne, Ypres, Loos, Festubert, Passchendaele and Bapaume. Rudyard Kipling wrote the official history of *The Irish Guards in The Great War* published in two volumes in 1923.

Gethsemane, page 111

After The Great War, 1914-18, Rudyard Kipling threw himself wholeheartedly into working for the Imperial War Graves Commission, although his only son Lieutenant John Kipling had no known grave. On the occasion of King George V's pilgrimage to war cemeteries in France in 1922, Kipling wrote, with heavy heart, '...*All they had they gave - they gave; and they shall not return, For these are those that have no grave where any heart may mourn...*'. In 1992 the Commonwealth War Graves Commission reported that after re-examining cemetery records they have now identified and marked Lt. John Kipling's grave at St. Mary's Advanced Dressing Station Cemetery, Haisnes, France.

Index of 1st Lines

Previous Publications

Postcard Sets

Volunteer Regiments of London
Military Units of Essex
The Royal Yeomanry
Regiments of Canada
17th/21st Lancers
Royal Canadian Mounted Police
Paintings by Lady Butler (1846–1933)
Grenadier Guards
London's Metropolitan Police
Kipling's Soldiers
French Foreign legion
R.A.F. Aircrew Clothing 1918–1988
Uniforms of the British Empire 1897
Paintings by R. Caton Woodville (1856–1927)
Uniforms of the Royal Navy
Italian Carabinieri
Military Art of Harry Payne (1858–1927)
United States Marine Corps
New York City Police Department
Corps of Royal Military Police
Inns of Court Regiment
The Black Watch (Royal Highland Regiment)
London Fire Brigade
Royal Scots Dragoon Guards
Scots Guards
American–Indian Wars
The Essex Regiment

Credits
Photographs

All the Black and White Photographs and
drawings in this book have been provided by
Peter Newark's Military Pictures, Bath, England.